JULIE L. TAYLOR

~ Kids ~
Don't Come With A
handbook, Handbook!

BALBOA.PRESS
A DIVISION OF HAY HOUSE

Balboa Press books may be ordered through booksellers or by contacting:

Balboa Press
A Division of Hay House
1663 Liberty Drive
Bloomington, IN 47403
www.balboapress.com
844-682-1282

Print information available on the last page.

ISBN: 978-1-9822-5888-7 (sc)
ISBN: 978-1-9822-5889-4 (e)

Balboa Press rev. date: 12/30/2020

The light & joys in my life...

– For Chase, Peyton, Corbin and Brock

*A guide for all parents - with some insightful answers
* to your mind-boggling questions

no-nonsense parental-good common sense practical advice

*Recipe for a happy-healthy relationship between kids and adults:
Patience, love, laughter, attention & forgiveness

Book was written when they were young... and NOW still applies today sharing it with the world.

A powerful parenting tool for all ages.

ABOUT THE AUTHOR

Born in LA raised in Utah, Julie is a mom of 4 boys who writes about her success in raising confident, happy, healthy, smart and independent children. Julie now shares the secret ingredients of powerful long lasting parenting.

She's also an author of "A Soul's Journey of Love" and the current reigning Ms. Hawaii USA Universal 2020/2021 (former Miss Hawaii USA & Mrs. Hawaii America).

A recipient of a Governors Award for Outstanding Community Service in Hawaii; World Traveler; Singer/Entertainer/Presenter. She is a lifelong advocate for children.

Julie is now a Women's Empowerment Coach & Leader with Inspire & Shine Bright Inspirational Intuitive Coaching. (Self Love, Honor, Value and Respect).

"talk"

100 *LISTEN

- Respond
- Explain... (age appropriate)

Babies cry for a reason ... try to be patient and do all you can. (hungry, dirty diaper, tired, lonely, afraid - just need to be held) * <u>Feed on demand</u>!

older: explain reasons for decisions.

99 *THEY'RE BORN THAT WAY ... (SO IT SEEMS)

With their own personality-character it seems. And it carries on throughout the years. - (changing slightly-maturing-adapting)

Enjoy their own individual uniqueness. (even when it's different from your own.)

98 *TAKE IT AS IT COMES

Babies - kids - adolescents - (teenagers) "Aaahhh"!

"Life"
go with the flow - and you won't lose control. (too much anyways)

<u>97</u> *GO WITH YOUR HEART ... (GUT-FEELING)

Head or your heart?
        <u>Both</u>
but, lean toward your heart.- for decisions. (you'll come out ahead)
-Things also seem to work themselves out-
*promptings-intuitions-impulses-instincts

<u>96</u> *LIVE AND LEARN

BUT
Don't ignore major problems or issues
Mistakes are all apart of it all .... remember that. Guilt - be gone
Learn from it!!!
then move on
don't waste precious time - deal with it.

1

95 *CHOICES ...... #1 (RESPECT)

Everybody responds better.

SO important!
give them choices!
it's <u>GOOD</u> for everyone
teaches them so much
responsibility-independence-confidence-trust

time
energy
patience
love

94 *TIME

Time is all we have
Time is on your side
give it some time
take the time!
Time heals
Time to begin

it's time to start - *making time!

93 *SPEAK UP

- and speak often
speak your peace
Do it with love & compassion and then vice versa
Learn to really listen
acknowledge-validate feelings,
*much easier this way!

92 * CHANGES

Having children is a <u>huge</u> change - no more just yourself to think about!

<u>"Responsibility"</u>

Staring you in the face. But, changes are <u>good</u>!
real good - inevitable. Deal with it positively.

91 * TEACH

don't preach -
they hear you!
Rules-Boundaries-<u>Yes</u>
But too rigid - no they may tend to rebel
Test you - yes
Consistency - your best bet.

90 *GET DOWN & DIRTY

Play with them. Let them explore. The kitchen floor/counter - food play <u>or</u> the great outdoors - it's fun for all! Clean up can be too ....

89 *MAKE IT A GOOD YEAR

*Explore world together
Make it a "good day. Each and every morning - positive outlook - thinking - required - it's a choice - remember that! It'll help tons!

88 *DOUBLE THE FUN

- two plus kids - awesome "playmates"
sibling support too ...

- Host get-togethers
"open-house" theory - open up your home - then you'll know where your kids are.

87 *CHORES

IT TEACHES ...
great for everyone!
everybody lives there - "everybody" needs to help out & pitch in ....
Mom's not the slave or the maid (though you feel you are at times)
Teach now/all ages can help!

eg...
eg...
eg...

86 *EXAMPLE

The five senses ...
They hear - they see - they know! Don't fool yourself. They're smart little people. So, be careful and teach by <u>example</u>. Remember - they're watching and learning. So - lead, guide, teach, learn & grow together positively.

85 *LOTS OF SNACKS

They get "<u>hungry</u>" alot!
Don't deprive them - (Don't let go to bed hungry.)
Choices are good, but healthy eating is a lifetime habit - treats are their icing on the cake ... And O.K.!

84 *REST ... (KEEP UP ONLY WITH YOURSELF. *DON'T WORRY ABOUT THE JONES

Zzzzz

not that you'll get much initially or even later on - but try to get some. All of you! very important for your health, alertness an attitude. Naps - time outs and bed-times are important at all ages really! Crankiness-not fun

83 *LOVE - TIME-ENERGY-PATIENCE

What you put into it (parenting and your family) is what you will get out of it! So, make it count!!

- Lots and lots of Love!
And patience
And your time

82 *WHAT'S BEST?

"Mama knows best" - plus books-friends-grandparents, all of it helps <u>but</u> - use your own instincts/ideas, it's a learned job/experience. Take what you like - out with the rest.
- On "feeding" - *<u>Breast is best!!! If can.</u>

81 *BEHAVIORS

reward good - not bad, make good-wise-smart decisions that help yourself and others, not ones that hurt or hinder. [Positive approach to all...]
teach with love, kindness, acceptance & patience
    by example ...

80 *PEER PRESSURE DRUGS ...(SEX)

It's real-talk about it! Even early on .... (age appropriate of course for information given)
"Aware"
this includes sexual areas and conversations, we're all sexual .... at all ages-really.

79 *CHANCES

WE all deserve 2nd chances! Allow for mistakes - learned lessons - a life-time thing.
What's key here?
*-Goal: learn from it/don't repeat!

78 *THEY'RE STILL YOUNG

So remember that! Still learning & growing. It's all new - to everyone
(you included)
All ages
All phases
* make it fun!

77 *½ THE BATTLE

is just "DOING"!
Doing, trying, loving & giving is an "ACTION" - A verb.

Just keep on going ...

<u>76</u> *TRUST & RESPECT

It's
it's a learned & <u>EARNED</u> thing.
(All ages) allow some freedoms.
<u>infants</u> - By your responding to their needs.
<u>older</u> - by how you treat them - support them - acknowledge & be there for them.

<u>75</u> *THREE QUARTERS

Sometimes it seems as if you give the majority of your time, efforts, energies and commitment in a parenting-child relationship, especially if your the female. (it seems in most cases)
Don't fret -
"ASK" for more help! 2-way street (give and take)

<u>74</u> *SPOUSAL SUPPORT ... ("<u>IN THE HOME</u>" OR OUT)

- Whether married or single
Support of ALL KINDS & areas - are very important & necessary.
* it takes 2 to tangle & two to be <u>responsible</u> too.
Hopefully - everyone steps up to the plate.

<u>73</u> *PRIORITIES ... (OTHERS TO THINK ABOUT - ALWAYS)

*Keep them in line!
The foundation of this nation are families. Families are there for you - people you can count on - (hopefully) that's the way it should be. It's not just for "you" anymore.

72 *BEST-SELF

- help them as well as yourself find your best-selves!
*By doing good.
Thinking good & positive things. Putting out your best self. Thinking good about yourself & those around you & what you are doing.

71 *ATMOSPHERE

Create a safe-loving-nurturing and positive - peaceful environment.
*Everyone will thrive in this kind of environment, in all areas and ways. A little effort goes along ways ... Keep it simple.

70 *SPIRITUALITY ... SET FOUNDATION/LATER THEY CAN DECIDE FOR THEMSELVES

- Whether in an organized religion or other-vitally important.

everyone questions   before's

during's

&

afters

put their minds at rest - not fill with guilt-shame or fear!

69 *GUIDELINES

Guidelines will help them in life - during child-rearing years as well as in future settings (jobs-situations-different scenarios.)

Gives sense of direction (security)

68 *GROOMING/HYGIENE

It starts early -
A lifetime habit
Confidence & self-esteem plays a big part in this area. (through the years)
Care .... and they will too!

67 *10 POSITIVES TO 1 NEGATIVE

Good job!
Well done!
Your terrific!

PRAISE your children often!!! (as well as yourself too ...)

Your wonderful - your special - your doing great! I'm proud of you - way to go.

66 *IT'S O.K. TO SAY NO

And to stick to it too
Boundaries-guidelines-rules consistency!
There are exceptions - of course!
("Yes" is nice too)
*SAFETY FIRST! Always

65 *CELEBRATE ... THEY'RE SPECIAL

Your child's life! They're important - so let them know it every chance you get. Make times together special, plus holidays/birthdays/family outings & traditions.

64 *PREPAREDNESS ... (IS THE KEY)

Come what may.
Open-heart/open mind

Kids are full of surprises
Prepare in advance - surprise/bad language
Prepare outings: extra clothes, snacks, diapers & drinks

63 *EXERCISE

For body-spirit-mind and even a break.
Running around with and after your kids is a great stay in shape activity.
Fun too! And exhausting!

62 *CARE

You care - so show it!
They care - so respond to their feelings - acknowledge

"Dare to Care"
When you love & feel loved - you care ...

61 *PLAN FOR TODAY & TOMORROW

But "LIVE" in the moment because that is all we really have, so - make the best of it right now! What's really important in your life??

60 *OPEN COMMUNICATION (-"CALM"-)

Keep the lines "OPEN"!

Don't explode (know it's hard sometimes not to) BUT
"Listen" breathe -
Count (to self) - leave room if you must
But talk about things!

59 *IF IT IS TO BE - IT IS UP TO ME!

It all starts with YOURSELF
Changes within-effect everything/one outwardly.

58 *DON'T KNOW WHICH WAY TO GO?

But there are a thousand roads to choose from ...

OPTIONS CHOICES - ALWAYS
But consequences as well - good or bad.

57 *CENTER OF ATTENTION

We all desire it sometimes especially kids!
There's a time and a place for everything - serious or fun & games,
but children should & need to be #1 in our eyes & theirs.

56 *RESPECTFUL

Courteous-kind-well-mannered

We all need to be these things no matter the age.
Be respectful to one another. We all prosper in this atmosphere.

55 *TAKE A BREAK

*everyone needs them now & again.
switch off .... get help.
Child-rearing is a 24-7 job, it truly is!
even more so, if your a full-time parent, but this period in time has
so many benefits-goes by so fast and leaves a legacy.

54 *LET THEM KNOW THEY ARE LOVED

Tell them- show them how much they are loved by you and everyone. They need to feel loved & secure. Let them know how much they mean to you & how you appreciate them.

53 *SOAP OPERA

Life can be like a soap opera - twists and turns, ups and downs, hills and valleys. Just hang in there - and never give up on yourself or them. Your all worth it and deserve the very best.

52 *HONESTY ... (LOYALTY)

Is not overrated.
Honesty-integrity-morals-values-standards.
*Great character!
Teach these traits by your own example.
It means so MUCH

51 *BUDGET ... (LIVE WITHIN YOUR MEANS!) NOT TO IMPRESS

WISELY!!!
Don't just blow it.
Bills first/don't get in over your head.
"NEEDS" over wants!!! (Thrift shop-it's fun...)
extras: savings & some play!
*important too!

50 *HALF-WAY THERE

Your half way there - DON'T GIVE UP! *Attitude
Set your mind and sights on the goal and stick to it - whatever it may be. Cup ½ empty or ½ full - outlook/viewpoint

49 *SELF-CONTROL

(Don't take it out on the kids)
Everyone gets a little testy here and there, but a little self-control goes along ways indeed.
Frustrated?
take breaks! Get help.
relax-calm-chill-de-stress.
however you can ... walks-baths

48 *BELIEVE

In yourself - your children and what you are doing. Believe it is possible ...

                        Anything

Faith - hope and belief ...
*We are all powerful spiritual beings!

47 *ALLOWANCES

equals: learned $ values - responsibility - self worth - self-esteem - independence - help with chores - learned life lessons really ...
*Incentives motivate
Keep practical

46 *LITTLE THINGS

Do little things each day to make each other "feel" special. Everyone needs some attention now and again
The saying: Kids are to be seen and not heard - Bull-pucky throw it out!

45 *GOALS

SET THEM - WRITE THEM DOWN - TALK ABOUT THEM.

Help your children to set and reach they're own.
                    encourage & support them
Perseverance!
We live & learn - kids will watch & learn ...

44 *ONE DAY AT A TIME

Sometimes that's all you can do & give.
Take it as it comes.
Direct your ship - set the sails and the course for "adventures" to come. Life is good overall. Be positive ....

43 *SPACE

everyone needs it occasional-even kids. Allow them to have their personal time (& space).

to think	to refocus
to pamper	to re-do
to relax	to plan
to recharge	to make better or right!
to READ	

42 *PARENTS DISCRETION ... (CUZ YOU LOVE & CARE ABOUT THEM)

television-movies-friends-curfews-etc...

set-stick to it-explain reasons (not "just because comments")
remember: your the parent! (you decide)

41 *MAKE YOUR HOUSE A HOME

Fill it with lots of love. Make a difference in your life as well as theirs.
*Enhance the quality of life right at home.

40 *ROLE MODEL

They are apart of you and they know it! Be the best example you can
be - as a wife, mother, father, husband, parent, worker and friend.
Thoughtfulness & integrity counts. Hugely

39 *GIVE

of yourself and your love freely - <u>unconditionally</u>!!!

give of your time - *** so very important!!!

Give choices too! Very good teaching tool!

38 *BE FLEXIBLE

Adaptable too ... your kids pick up <u>a lot</u> from you and also decide to "change" things within themselves that they would like to do differently later on in life -(it's not all set in stone - a give & take of energies.)
(and that's O.K.)

37 *EVERYONE IS DIFFERENT

just because you or someone else - including myself says this is the way - it doesn't necessarily works for everyone and may not be the only way. There is NO 1 (one) way.
Options - other ways & choices exist.

36 *ENJOY IT ALL

each phase and age is so completely different and wonderful as well
as challenging in their own ways. Take it all in. Live it fully.
- Time is ticking -
So just kick back - relax & enjoy.

35 *CONFLICTS ... -(TALK IT OUT)

Yes- they do happen.
Deal with it - resolve - and move on.
Dwelling on it - not good for anyone.
Put past in past, motivate self & others to move on & forward ...
*A new day begins.

34 *WATCH THEM CLOSELY!!!

Things can happen quickly!
(All ages really)

run-off
kidnapped
in trouble with the law
involved with substances
etc... etc...

33 *ACCEPT HELP ... (GRACIOUSLY)

We think we can & should do it all - but sometimes we just can't do it all - all of the time. (cup & plate overloaded - overfilled - "overwhelmed")

EVERYONE in household needs to pitch in and help. See what needs to be done & just do it - *Ask how help too...

32 *IN YOUR CHILDREN'S EYES

There is love-hope-faith-joy-laughter and forgiveness.

They are God's greatest of gifts!!! Learn from them & cherish them...

31 *AN OUNCE OF PREVENTION IS WORTH A POUND OF CURE

That old & wise saying - very true!
Stop any negativity before it begins.
Be aware - ask questions - step in - make necessary changes.

30 *LAUGH - JOKE

Have fun!!!
Life's too short enjoy it - enjoy each other! Don't take everything <u>so</u> seriously. Let your hair down.

29 *SMILE

proven to make you <u>"feel"</u> better and look better too. Find/Look/ Feel the goodness and joy in each and every day no matter your toils. Lighten the load with a smile.

(De-stress)

28 *DON'T TAKE IT PERSONALLY

people react
kids react
allow kids to express their feelings - important not to bottle up - but release constructively (otherwise resentments/rebel?) problems
Learn to let things go ...

27 *KIDS ARE MUCH SMARTER THAN YOU THINK

Hey, they came from you - what do you expect. They'll take all the good things from you and your left with more love than you can possibly imagine. NOTHING compares ...

26 *MANNERS ... *(TEACH... AND EXPECT) RESPECT!

Ladies and young gentlemen
not a thing of the past - still very important. Help them to realize that yes it does matter. (How they act-behave-speak-school etc...)

25 *LET THEM FEEL VALUED

Because they are! You can't spoil an infant or a child of any age with lots & lots of "LOVE".

*Kids are so very special in every way!

24 *ONE ON ONE TIME

as a couple (if ... a couple) as well as with each child as much as possible, (important and needed.)
love them equally ....

23 *FUN-FUN-FUN

Kids are just plain & simply fun!
even when it gets wild & crazy
try to seize the moment-for one day it'll be gone. See the humor in things. (as much as possible)

22 *BE KIND

"unwind" - yourself (better for everyone) from everyday pressures of work - home & life (leave work at work)
if stressed - stop & think breaks ...
[separate]

21 *NO WORRIES

whether your young ones are 21 months or 21 years of age - rest assured you've done well in your parenting. After all the lessons - guidance & direction they are in fact their own little people/person. (own path)
Advice/support they still need you.

20 *LET THEM PLAY ... -SOCIALIZATION

Their play is their work
        and
Their work is their play.

Play with them, get down on their level, see the world through their eyes, whatever their age ... Participate!!!

19 *ESTABLISH A SET OF VALUES

in your home, family & life.

Chances are they will carry it with them through life... And that's a good thing. Helps in all aspects of life.

18 *SAFE & SECURE

Children need to know and feel that they are SAFE & SECURE. Even with changes and all ...
STABILITY in some things - a "constant" is reassuring.
Teach & practice safety & cautionary measures.
Better safe than not ...

17 *DATES

Family night (schedule it in)

togetherness is vitally important! (Take & make the time)

you'll be glad you did. It makes the world of difference in your relationships with spouse and kids!

16 *SWEET SIXTEEN ... (JUST GO WITH THE FLOW)

At 16 months - walking, starting to talk well, learning so much & growing so fast.
or
At 16 years of age - seeking independence, driving a car, going out, being with friends - even getting a job. It's all O.K.

15 *SPONTANEITY

It's fun! Adventurous! Unscheduled. Unleashed in a way from daily routines (which are good!)

But - everybody needs or should enjoy some spontaneity at times. Last minute plannings - outings happenings. Spice of life.

14 *DO AND GIVE UNTO OTHERS

as you would want others to do unto you!
                    - The Golden Rule -
Show & teach your children how good it is & how good it feels to treat others kindly & with respect. (Give of yourself.)

13 *IF AT FIRST YOU DON'T SUCCEED

try & try again. ["Do-over"]
        Just "DO"!
Don't stop ...
Find the way in each and every new day. Ask for guidance from up Above!

12 *ENCOURAGEMENT - ACCEPTANCE

Acceptance - of self & others
Encouragement - of each other

Motivate & inspire the best & better self of one another. Look for the good.

11 *OPEN DOOR POLICY... (BE INTERESTED ...)

Let them know they can always come to you - talk to you - trust you - know they can always count on you. (to talk-listen-understand-help-be there for them ...)

*Listen-listen-listen to your children ....

10 *FOCUS IN ON YOUR CHILDREN

Their needs
    wants
    goals
    dreams & desires
*Tell them they can do anything they put their minds to. Help them however you can, to achieve them. Your there to "HELP" them - "LOVE" them .... *(Be there for them)

<u>9</u> *YOU CAN BE THEIR "HERO"

Yes - in so many ways (But let them learn on their own too)
(younger children especially - but all ages and sometimes it takes
until adulthood/parenthood for them to see & realize all you tried
to do for them) not an easy task - But so worth it! In so many ways ...

<u>8</u> *TOUGH LOVE ... (BECAUSE YOU CARE.)

apply when needed and appropriate...

But never ever remove or take away your love. Unconditional love -
never-ending love - A parents love is a given!

<u>7</u> *FAMILIES ARE FOREVER

so they say - Believe! And in your heart - so do you probably. (already)
Families may change - but the love you have for your children grows
& grows! Take care of each other.

<u>6</u> *PARENTING ROLES ... (BE PROUD TO BE A PARENT!)

Traditionally:
Mother: nurtures children
Father: provides/takes care of...
*still strong but-
- times changed - (for a %) everyone does their part to help out in
all areas.
*Focus in on "your" strengths ...

<u>5</u> *TRADITIONS

Keep up with them. They are the little things that really count - make
a difference - the things they remember and even maybe carry on .....
A part of you and your times together. So very special they are!

<u>4</u> *KIDS ARE GREAT ... *(LIFE CHANGING)

They are a hoot! Wild and crazy at times. Drive you insane sometimes.
But, HILARIOUS really. (especially when you look back.)
*Don't make a small thing huge.

<u>3</u> *GIVE YOURSELF A PAT ON THE BACK

every now and again you deserve it! It's not always easy - but oh so
very worth it! Just hang in there - all things will pass...

2 *"ENJOY"

GREAT ACCOMPLISHMENT
The ultimate ☺
        "ENJOY" them .... Be proud of them

* every hour - everyday - every moment. For one day they be gone .... all grown up and their own! And you did it .... Hurray!

1 *YOUR KIDS

- your pride and joy
They're the greatest things that will EVER happen to you! Guaranteed!!!!
*Tell them you love them

1 *YOUR FAMILY

- your laughter & tears throughout all your years. (true blessings)

Be kind - Be wise - Be careful - Be mindful - Be loving and gentle - Be understanding and mostly. Just BE THERE .....

NOTES

Last minute pointers ...

* Keep your chin up!
* Hang in there ...

and most importantly -

just <u>love</u> and <u>enjoy</u> them! They're so worth it.